T0113782

Nuptials At Vespers
&
Other Strains
Poems

John Ngong Kum Ngong

Langaa Research & Publishing CIG
Mankon, Bamenda

Publisher:
Langaa RPCIG
Langaa Research & Publishing Common Initiative Group
P.O. Box 902 Mankon
Bamenda
North West Region
Cameroon
Langaagrp@gmail.com
www.langaa-rpcig.net

Distributed in and outside N. America by African Books Collective
orders@africanbookscollective.com
www.africanbookscollective.com

ISBN: 9956-792-10-1

DISCLAIMER
All views expressed in this publication are those of the author and do not necessarily reflect the views of Langaa RPCIG.

Table of Contents

Bootless Tussle

In vain have I struggled
not to put these lines down.
It has been ages now
since the battle started.
My every step to pluck
the hot heart of the poet
and throw it to the dogs
ended in depression.

The days went by weeping
bleeding driblets of red.
In vain I tried to slice
the sharp tongue of the bard
and toss it to the sharks.
I went into reverse
flung carvers and daggers
out from my hostile heart
and worked hard towards peace.
Swallows were witnesses.

We have become great friends
the beat bard and my me.
He has taught me his art
the bullheaded crack poet.
I try to hit the mark
each time he points the way
and sing a different song
whenever he conducts
to make sure we are one
for new voices to voice

concern about the lack
of concern amongst us.

Tomorrow when I am dust
the songs left behind would speak
of the violent wars we fought
the verse-maker and myself
against corruption and lies,
against oppression and theft
even if you fail to speak.
I want you to bear in mind
till the conclusion of time
this challenging train of thought
my rising star, not to die
in the flower of your age.
It cuts down my dignity
to drink from turbid waters.

Empty Pitcher

I drain my blows in songs
soaked in the wine of whine.
You can make game of me,
swing like a pendulum
in your seeming success
and ladle out your dross
to skin-and-bone writers
fighting to grow fat in darkness.

I am not a peasant
panting under a weight.
I am in the middle
struggling to make a way
along which the middle,
the peasant and the blind
can thrive like hibiscus
sometimes in hostile surroundings.

I am not upper class
breathing down the people.
I am in the middle
struggling to break the wall
that for these gruesome years
has kept us asunder
fragmented, colourless,
vulnerable and numb with fear.

I drain my blows in thought
dipped in the sauce of lore
anywhere in the land.

You can make sport of me
to quench your rage with blood
and roll in your vomit.
The land is full of fibs
forged in your brand new forge
to forge ahead with plans
to forge our country's seal
for francs from our forests.
You do not think of me
when your purse is swollen.
You do not rush to me
when pus drips in my heart.
You are cert an empty pitcher.

Welcome

With open arms and clear mind
I welcome you to my grounds
where for these unnumbered years
I have labored like white ants.
The pillars of shame still stand
in the middle of the yard
where you and I tied the knot
against the dreams of kinsmen.

I welcome you great thinkers
to this place of great marvels
where for a long period now
my heart and mind like twin drums
beating in the square of death
wait for a cute catch, great minds.
The people need bread and oil
to gather and share like ants.
Great minds ought to oust lean thoughts
and smash the head of terror.

Lost in multiplex thoughts
in the coldness of my world
the music of ants mocks me.
I neither can sing like them
nor gather the food they fetch.
The easy resort to threats
bangs on the door of my heart
furious, trembling like water
boiling over hot fire.
I will not pick a quarrel

in the womb of emotion
to build a name unworthy.

Welcome to my territory
where I am giving my all
to close the page of done days
with a will for the morrow.
I roll out my old carpet
for you and your acolytes
haunted by disappointment.
I am like you in the cold
beating self for the mishmash
creating tension in my head.
Your coming could change my fate
at the turn of the corner
before I come to nothing.
Welcome chip off the old block.

Nuptials at Vespers

We got hitched many years back
where a Dragon with twin tongues
the emblem of the people
tracks your coming and leaving.
The rains were severe that day
and the wild winds inclement
but the nuptials still took place.

The officiating Mayor
gawky but sparkling like wine
sealed the union at vespers
smiling at the thought of loot.
The link room was boiling hot,
the masses outside went wild
and the Mayor the bull yelled.

We wined and dined steeped in guile
till midnight that fateful day.
I endured pain to love you
in season out of season
and my breasts yearned for your touch.
I thirsted for truth and warmth
but got bottles of red wine.

Feckless Spouse

My husband does not mind me
nor the bees in his cornfield
nor the dead nor the red wasps
hanging over him like death.
He does not prize me at all
because his mind roams and roams
in the yard of grey grandeur
looking for a cap that fits.
Man is such a foul creature.

The Mayor lies in the room
where he pressed us exchange rings.
Beetles bore holes in his head
and hatred in dark glasses
spits on his grey beard in dust.
I care not what your songs say
but I know they will never
sing the rise of a new breed
with metaphors that wrestle.
Man leans and breaks bread on man.

My husband does not like me
nor the dreams nor the children
shadowing him in his dreams
but I will sing of his love
which for years flooded my eyes
and spilled my blood to cry wolf.
For tomorrow I will sing
of men with elegant hearts
ready to captain our youths

to build without spilling blood.
I will sing of men with spines.

Prison

A thousand and one storms
have for these many years
swept over our wedlock
my proud careless husband.
I have borne with sang-froid
your misuse without sleep
far far into the night.

Today I sleep at death's door
emptied of my dignity,
dying to give you the slip
from this prison called coupling
without punches without blood.
I can no longer withstand
with the heart of a mortal
the prickles in your embrace
and the whisky in your breath.

I prefer to be my nothing
where I can sing and dance freely,
think constructively with friends
living within my meager means.
If the price I must pay for love
be my upfront tongue so be it.
I cannot tell lies to lie with
masquerades on beds of gold.
The murderous look in your eyes
will not stop me from speaking out
for the world to see your fealty.

You are afraid of losing my milk
not my affection and devotion.
I prefer to be my nothing still
where the bones of my progenitors
unbiased and sincere rest in peace.
Let me go back to where they settled
in the nitty-gritty of justice
where hearts are not tainted with envy.
Stop shedding tears like a crocodile
lying in wait for prey to devour.
You have no right eating from my dish
and drinking my milk without working
conceited and unproductive spouse.

Stupid Love

Love is so stubborn and stupid
without direction now and then.
Love is an intriguing monster
with fangs formed to tear and deform
hearts without roots and bonfire
to burn the lies of lewd leopards
and the garments of ravishers.

I want to see my Bull knackered
before my love with contusions
listens to cantatas of hope
without the rantings of drunk dogs.
I want to see him genuflect
before my beloved on crutches
sits down to cut and thrust with him
where we accepted to be one.

I do not want to see midgets
or people without strong voices.
I want to see all the young men
of this rum country rise up strong
with reins like those of grown horses
before my done body grows cold
in the tireless mouth of Death
ready to devour one at once
for worms to grow fat and happy.
Love is so stubborn and stupid
without circumspection sometimes.
It has plagued me these many years
and painted my ego gloomy.

I want my head to lead me now
away from the sway of the heart
and a wrong administration
sloppy and undependable
as intermittent snaky streams
to do repairs in my torn heart.

Take Me Back

I can no longer stand it
the way you cash in on me.
Come with me to the Mayor
on the eve of the next rains.
I do not want to wangle
or break faith as others do
in many parts of the world.
I do not want to rob too
or watch the blood of our sweat
oil the wheels of corruption.

I can no longer bear it
the way you put me to use.
Take me back to the Mayor
before knife thoughts take over.
I am sick of crushing hands
in my bid to save the rights
enslaved many years ago
by my lack of discernment.
I do not want to die lame
or tread the earth like a ghost
with scarlet thorns in my heart.

Nausea scrapes with obsession
the lining of my stomach
like a woman scrubs a pot
coated with soot thick as clay.
The moonshine of my conscience
tapers off day after day
and the skin of my aura

has lost its fair complexion.
I can no longer stomach
the sight of your trenchant tongue
nor sit serene on your laps
now like the back of a frog.

Cut to the Quick

Let me wipe dry your tears
watching our kids kill time
as the sun goes to sleep
and the heat shadows us.
Tonight might be ice cold
but mosquitoes will be hot.
Our highly endowed statesmen
decked in foreign outfit forge
distant from the swelling screams
and the call of the dying.

Let me wipe clean my hat
for a short pleasure trip
as the sun wakes from sleep
and the downhearted yawn.
Today might be splendid
though the smell of rot still rules
giving chase to dying flesh
in the heart of the city.
I will clog my keen nostrils
to count all the rotting trunks
in the foul streets and drinking spots
to feel better in my done bones.

Call to mind who we are
and where we all come from.
Refuse was revolting,
an unwelcome tenant
rotten to the kernel.
In this day and age, mean mouths

and slimy tongues tongue the praise
of corrupt festering souls
and bungled democracy.
Cut to the quick, I spend days
in my murky moth-eaten shack
giving suck to young rescuers.
We without question are not pigs
at ease in mud munching dead cats.

Celebrating Tenderness

Rub my feet my beloved
with camwood from the hills.
Set to music the lines
I wrote under the rocks
when I had not yet learnt
how to arrive at will
like the rose in my bed
celebrating your tenderness.

Prepare my foofoo dear
with cornflour from home.
Let the songs I last wrote
return to us the breathe
lost trying to teach dogs
to bark and bite in time
when the scent of the foe
crawls near the roof over our heads.

I am in a river
shallow flowing uphill
towards my ancestry.
I wait for the daystar
and the songs in your eyes
to face what lies ahead.
I pledge to continue
celebrating your tenderness.
Rub my feet my beloved
with the real camwood from home.
Set to music the lines
I wrote in the river

when the fire of lust
charred the bloom in my mind
celebrating your tenderness.

Memorable Journey

I embarked on a journey,
a memorable journey
from the steep hills of Esu
through the plains of Great Soppo
to the centre of great thought.
I saw the mysterious Mungo
whose brown waters unsuspicious
flow gently as if enchanted.
Anyone who tries to jump in
without a right lifejacket drowns.

I crossed to the other side
of the river filled with hope,
anxious to start life anew
but my mind staged a revolt
and the rains came unannounced.
In spite of this I settled down
hoping to straighten out my ways
to work with a patriotic heart
together with the folk this way
for Cameroon to touch the world.

I will not mourn the demise
and the last hour of my clash
with the gods of the Mungo.
I will not mourn at my age
nor sit around rusty minds.
I will swell the womb of furore
and my offspring like a lion
will tear to bits politicians.

They will come like a pent-up flood
and sweep away carrion canon.

You Cannot Understand

You cannot understand,
might never understand
the motives that bind me
to this bleeding terrain
even at your ripe old age.
You cannot really understand
why my heart goes out for this land.

You have to dig deep deep
into the heart of love
to guess why I still breathe.
The ground here soft and fat
takes delight in my thinking.
The fauna and the flora here
love the interest I take in them.

Conflict often arises
when the rains stop kissing earth.
Sometimes loneliness creeps in
just when the heart wants to smile.
I have seen horrible things
and followed as a widow
walking after the bier
the remains of dead bodies
without heads without sex members.

Remorse has wrapped its cold hands
round my eager to help soul
showering it with kisses
more than human tongue can tell.

Give full vent to your anger
if that will make your seed grow
to become as strong as death
and flourish like a palm tree
here where real producers get lost.
I cannot abandon my country
just to catch a glimpse of liberty.

Sinister System

I seasoned, sealed up with fear,
always forcing a faint smile
dressed in immaculate white
to placate my hell-born boss
and singe his bushy eyebrows
in our sinister system.

I broke the ludicrous seal,
threw the pieces in the pit
my blood dug in my conscience
battered but not checkmated.
I know my boss cannot suss
why I am so hard to peel
like getting blood from a stone.
The system has seasoned me.

Lost in the bowels of power
my boss wears out the day cursing
concocting from the depths of spleen
poison gas for subversive tongues.
I want to enter his strange heart
to learn to kiss the crack of whips
and chop my way through undergrowth
to grow wiser in the darkness
that cuts to the bone the longing
to chop spite like meat for the pot.

Cross your heart beloved fatherland
looking out on the rising sun
not to mourn like a dripping owl

when my destiny comes unstuck
and my corse along with my cause
come in search of a resting place.
Turn your face cherished motherland
towards my depreciating frame
fumbling in the dark with feelings
fishing for my destiny key.
It is the keenness in your voice
that keeps my spirits on the beam.

No Place to Carve

The raw coldness these days
cuts the lobes of my heart.
The coldness in your voice
and the fear in folks' eyes
blunt the urge to sunder
the cord that hitches us
to boneheads elbowed up
the palm tree of power.
I do not know whether
my bones will stand the spell
without you my warm wind
winding along my tracks.

Neither songs from my flute
as old as the mountains
nor the sting of scorpions
can move nefarious souls
or unseat the old fox
playing dice with our lives.
In a dream I see you
wearing the hat of change
deaf to what people say
in the red chains of change
charring but not falling,
burning but not dying.

At my arthritic age
in this place of scandals
where the most gifted fade
and the talentless shine

I want my name printed
on the front page of change.
What I want at my age
is the honour I wore
before the senile fox
taught me to wear a mask
holding to ransom truth
wrapped in euros and francs.

This is no place to carve
the name of your idol
where the head wears its wreath
like a king in power.
This is no place to raise
a statue of self-rule
out of our bent history.
This is where you can steal
cut off from the people
to steel yourself to cheat.
This is where grey dogs thrive
eating the dugs of hags.

Minds in the Wilderness

At the window of my mind
in the small hours of the day
I looked out through the netting
my heart gone out to the homeless.
I saw among the masses
gathered around a strange man,
a young man who lacked lodging
struggling to catch the man's eye.

Unsuccessful in his bid
the young man gave way to tears
hoping to attract the crowd.
Nobody took the trouble
to turn and listen to him
cry the names of missing friends.
The strange man said something sore
about big names without loins.

The young man stopped lamenting
but the hurdles of his life
a thousand and one of them
fought a pitched battle with him.
Stabbed, he crawled into himself
afraid to join the people
gathered around a queer man
a cutthroat rage in their eyes.
For some strange troubling reason
the people made sign language,
their minds in the wilderness.
Their licentious souls drank in

with zest the foreigner's lies.
My mind upset, fell asleep
under the stool in my head.
Flustered I shut the window.

Refusing To See

Why should I bother my brains
for folks who refuse to see
the column of coal-black smoke
drifting across the country?
Why should I look upon them
dipsticks who have dimmed my art
and put under lock and key
those who should have wrestled on,
those who should have rung the gong
to keep the state from choking?

Though deep in the mouth of mould
howling my goggle eyes out
in the darkness of my life
as the smoke sails through the land,
though walking with my head bowed
through streets lined with detractors
the day is coming, rushing
like wind preceding a storm.
Though hunted like a rat mole
my songs shall someday search you.

It is not dignifying
to be denied deserved dues
or to be stripped by bastards
licensed to shave bare our land
singing the dirge every year
in a never ending night.
Even though on the breadline
because born on the wrong side

I will tear the veil of shame
drawn over my human traits
since I leaped from my mum's womb
a string strung around my neck.
I will take the young somewhere
under the wing of the Muse
to break the arm of bondage.

Wrestling Match

This surly song I sing
in the belly of drought
should neither depress you
nor rock your brains to sleep.
Life is not a straight line.

I have lived through dryness
scared without a stitch on
and crawled from my desert
to relieve my parched throat
in the slim stream near you.
Life is gloom to many.

Sometimes like a lizard
I nod my head thoughtful
and run across the yard
to capture a cockroach
to whet my appetite
before I start singing.
Life is a wrestling match.

I am aware of the bomb,
the time bomb in our bosom
waiting to explode someday
save justice rules otherwise
and politicians change cast.
Let nothing slip through your claws
as you wrestle with wild life.
Fight to make life meaningful.

There is nothing you do not know
and there is nothing worth the salt
in the snake tongues of demagogues.
I have many a time let things slip
and given ruthless dogs the slip
to cultivate a straight image
for our heirs never to forget
their roots in darkness and in night.
Never give up when life taunts you.

Wounded by the talons of time
and barely daring to give tongue
to the white elephants we praise,
the lord of the rack and the screw
thinks I should be stripped of my brains.
As I give thought to such base thought
a bird lands in my heart singing
the death of my coldblooded boss.
Give impenitent life no room
to put your back down in the dust.

Speaking One Language

On the hills of my heart
I kiss your blushing breasts
asleep on the dwarf bed
we bought last dry season
near where the woods are dead.
Open your mind to me
as I inearth all doubts.

I sit and watch you work
your heart buried in books,
books about love and tears
books about fear and guts
books about birth and death
in the heart of the day
as I trace your coming.
I give you my body.
In the womb of my breast
with my grey-speckled hair
I lie still on your breasts
chewing the nuts of love
we cracked when still blooming.
Let the light in your eyes
flood my blood with light
and the dream on your face
fill the drums in my heart.

I lie and watch you laugh
your mouth streaming fragrance
that drives my nose crazy
and sinks into my heart

like shards of broken glass.
Leave your books on the ground
near my earliest footprints.
Turn the page of the past
in this slippery place
even after the rains.

In a land of shadows
where the smell of candour
is a stalking leopard
and darkness rules the day
we must speak one language
as thunder and lightning.
The wind rushes past us
whistling unnerving tunes.
Our hearts must speak one tongue
to tie the hands of ruin
and fight to remain one.

Awaken The Giant

Many tongues have to be slashed
to stem the tide of rising
rising slowly in our blood.
They make those in power sick
and cause the weak to tremble
afraid to be lashed like thieves.

Dry the cold sweat in your eyes
to break the yoke on our necks
and crush the balls of silence
to awaken the giant
in the heart of everyone
who loves this groggy country.
Dry the cold sweat in your eyes
to swim to the shore of freemen.

This is no time to find fault
or ride through the city streets
in a cadillac of self.
The claws of tyranny tear
at our bosoms like a hawk
yet most of us seal our lips.
Stitching your mouth is to die
and be buried like an ass.
I am in torment within
because my mates are silent.

Race with my Thoughts

The atmosphere was heavy
like a woman big with child.
Relics of what used to gleam
in this part of the country
came flying like occultists
the day I stopped by the graves
of hands who for years labored
to drain the pus from our blood.

You may think I am stupid
stopping by colourless graves,
troubling the peace of silence
in a place too dry to weep.
I shall never feel at home
nor consider myself great
mending the skull of Cain.
I want to live like the moon.

Let me blow my aged whistle
in the ear of the old salt
you usually love to taste
on a bed of dead flowers.
Her blood and bites derail you
and like bamboo without pith
your head floats down sewage pipes.
It is hard to weep for you.

I shall try to jump through hoops
to pull the speck from your eye
and drain the sludge in your blood

in spite of my aged weak veins.
Believe me, I will not drop
the spade I use everyday
to dig people out of waste
though insane minds want you dead.

I run a race with my thoughts
every morning through wasteland,
counting the scant cypress trees
and the waterless stream beds
pleading with the rains to come.
Men at ease may keep silent.
I will speak to forestall ruin
and instill love for landscape.

Baffling

It was not a sight to behold
near a new building site downtown.
A child of ten gaunt and hungry
fell into a deep pit latrine.
The people around saw nothing,
they also understood nothing
when in their darkness they found out
a young man had drowned in faeces.

Indignation gripped me so tight
I was unable to breathe well.
I wish you could walk through my heart
to see the fresh crippling worries
drinking my old blood like palm wine.
I wish you could swear blind right now
you would allow in the homeless
and dust my plaint songs on your shelves.

Compelled by empathy's big stick
I dragged myself to the foul spot.
Alone I stood down in the mouth
but ready to rouse my muscles
to stand up and speed up succour.
I waited in the stench for long
for other large-hearted people
in this region of the country
where fellow-feeling breeds contempt
and the culprit rots in prison.

When darkness fell and the moon rose
I turned and left the place baffled.
There are laurels in the venture
of smashing a crocodile's eggs
and turning against a reptile,
himself a snatcher of our eggs.
In the parking lot of myself
I pushed my mind to the limit
to shut the door on the dead boy
and send crocodiles to the stake.

Do Something

Haggard from want and hopelessness,
compelled to sleep on dry stream beds
Kang like a plant torn from its home
staggers through harsh streets without base
bellowing like a bull gone nuts.

His heart carries a big burden,
a burden too heavy for him,
a burden beyond your prowess,
a burden politicians sneer
seated around a pot of cream.

I want you to say something fresh,
something to stop Kang from crashing.
Your silence increases his load
and the guilt we carry around
pretending to be patriotic.

We all suffer some injury
roaming the dark bright streets of life.
I wonder whether you see Kang
struggling hard not to waste away
like a garment eaten by moths.

I want you to do something great,
something to give Kang hope in drums.
Ignited with a solar flame
he would burn the dirt and the filth
robbing us of our amour propre.

Prepare Kang a place in your heart,
an airy and adequate room
where he can run to whenever
the heat of life burns his fingers
and predators plunge for his heart.

Our Duty

I see them combing the streets
looking for the eye of life
youths with cheeks carved out of need.
I feel like a dog with ticks
and my senses waver dim
as if my hurricane lamp
so dear will soon be snuffed out.

The tin god in high office
backed by bane politicians
proclaims the youths are artists
looking for the key to fame.
How they take us for a ride
these thieving politicians
ready to eat dung to shine.

Turn round and reason with me.
Turn round and look at those kids
deep in the bowels of dearth.
You must not take one more step
without stopping here with me
to give a hand to the youths
struggling to stitch their torn lives.

We have the duty to help them
heal the sore wounds in their bellies.
We have the duty to help them
sharpen the knives they have carried
since the day they perceived the sun.
We must assist them push their rage

into the heart of the tin god.

Let us look beyond the seasons
like our forefathers did singing.
Let us look beyond the seasons,
embrace what our hearts can embrace
and rubbish the rule of hatred.
I am in love with the fire
that still dances in your grey eyes.

Beast Of Prey

Like a lion in cover
you lie in wait everyday
to catch stranded animals.
Your face scintillates with fat,
the fat of your victims crushed
on their way to look for food.
My denunciation pours out
like water from a burst pipe
day to day to no avail.
Giving life no breathing space
you put out the lamp of hope
and rip your foes to pieces.

Houses crumble to rubble
and the earth kind as ever
receives the dead on cloud nine.
Dead and festering bitches
blasted in the night of want
where men like you dig their gold
are scattered about like snares.
I thought you could remember
that man is but a maggot.
Your brain is mistress to worms.
I must dig and plant new trees
lest I be stripped of my name.

The land is getting wilder
and you see only quarry
in the hearts of the confused.
The forests have been butchered

and houses have been burnt down.
Many lives have been taken
from animals and from man
to fill the pockets of rogues.
You pass by level terrain
to live where you can trail prey
and chop down trees at leisure
for a name in high places.

The Human Beast

When the beast in man gets mad
the heart looks for where to hide.
The mind jumps from mount to mount
in the hope of finding molten
to roast the beast in broad daylight.
Reason as usual struggles hard
not to soil its delicate hands
with the blood of partiality.

The beast has ruled us for long
clad in raw monstrosity.
The beast has eaten much lye
in the hope of keeping away
rivals from his belly kingdom.
Fear as usual struggles hard
not to stain this beautiful land
with the blood of innocent souls.

The beast and his acolytes
drunk with power like a hawk
will without doubt fall like leaves
dropping from an ant-eaten tree.
Their glory will certainly fade
like the crowns of unkempt flowers.
No matter how their dogs will bark
they will not scare away the crowd
bent on slicing lies and deception
like onions for the sauce of liberty.

My tears fall for the fallen
and a stab of loneliness
burns through my veins like fire.
Blotches of my failure to slash
the heads of snakes in sleeping suits
remain fresh in the sub-conscious.
I do not weave these weeping poems
to win your spineless approval.
I sing that those beaten down by life
may stand up and wrestle to live on.

Delusions of Grandeur

If the madness of politics
has taken a seat in your head
like a lion hungry for prey
climb the stone ladder beside you,
the one overlooking the deep.
Jump into the sea and fly-fish.
Maybe you will catch healthy fish
if the waves do not shatter you.

If the delusions of grandeur
and the folly of indifference
have started a home in your heart
like white ants in an anteroom,
scale the bone wall ahead of you,
the one adjoining the graveyard.
Burrow through the earth like a fox
perhaps you will find a real home.

Your octopus mentality
cuts the ground from under the feet
of dreamers on their way to build
a home of people with thick skins,
people to reshape our history.
I shall never fail to recall
the forged marriage certificate
you gave me promising fair play.
Delusions of grandeur like mice
have eaten your heart of love.

The years have flown past like the wind
sweeping coarse sand into my eyes.
My brain is still alert and brisk
keeping a weather eye on brains
bent on hawking our rights to hawks.
I want genuine marriage records,
the ones before the masquerade
after the Grassfield conference.
I do not see the reason why
I should live here bereft of light.

My Head

Heads are like greedy dogs
that never have enough.
They come to you like angels
black white red and yellow heads
but drain you of all your strength.
They come to you as servants
but empty what you have brewed.

I do not like my head
not because of its size
and the silver hair on it
but because it torments me.
When I was young it lured me
to a harbor without ships.
Now that I am brown like dust
with a skin eaten by time
my head still terrifies me.

Black white red and yellow heads
just like mine misuse power
and lead folks astray with lies.
They often harass great minds
and burden the populace
to build their names by deceit,
expand their rule by carnage
and exclude the hothead poet.
I hate my head like faeces
not because of its long bones
and the foreign caps it wears
but because it exploits me.

My head like a wayward child
that never stoops to listen
turns down cosmetics for its hair,
cosmetics processed from its sweat
in an obscure plant in Europe.
I hate my head like a dog's fart
because it loves only home cream.

Ungroomed Heads

In my marrow, in my blood,
everywhere in my inside
I feel the ceaseless movement,
the unbroken flow of shame
trickling down my failing legs.
Any day the flow may swell
like a stream with rain water
and drown the crabs in my mind
or sweep away years of hell
in the tents of ungroomed heads.

History will stitch up the wounds
we sustained digging the road
to the bedrock of justice
under ungroomed heartless heads.
My torn dresses will be patched
before I take to the road
for the last lap of my drive
through this clear as mud country.
My offspring will wear new clothes
and hold firm to what should be,
rule of law void of brute force.

You may gloat over my plight
as my bones grow weak daily.
Your mouth breathes out hellfire
like a dragon made with rage,
racing to and fro famished.
You can neither devour me
nor set fire to my stand

though I am like broken brick.
Beyond dispute you are dross
meet for the meat of vultures
moved up the ladder of sway
not by merit but by scam.

It is no feat to carouse
or beat the big beaded drum
you borrowed to drum your way
through moonless streets and lame minds.
It is no laughing matter
to sign up for parliament
riding on our smarting backs,
oblivious of our burden.
Your sting sticks like a fishbone
in my neighbour's bone dry throat
and threatens me at knifepoint.
I cannot betray my blood
to rise like an ungroomed head.

Living Without Your Head

You love to live without your head
in a world overwhelmed by guile
a world overrun by violence
a world where only tyranny
lined with bulletproof wears the crown.

You are not wet behind the ears
like a stranger to our past tense.
Everyone feels your recklessness
and we are in the main shaken
as trees are shaken by the wind.

You think I am as green as grass
in that the wretched of the land,
jewel in the crown of Elohim
gather in my home every day
to break unleavened bread with me.

Let my grey hair not deceive you
to sprout purple wings overnight
and fly away like an eagle
to perch on the fruit tree near me
thinking my fire has been doused.

Things are going to change hue soon
and people who wreck the nation
and reduce men to loaves of bread
would be pounded like cocoyams
and laid at the feet of warthogs.

You love to live without your head
in a world draped in corruption
dripping blood and atrocity
a world where you are contented
ever taking the second seat.

The World Breaks Everyone

The world breaks everyone,
the poor and the wealthy
the dull and the clever
the weak and the sturdy.
I hang out in the world
so am no exception.
It can break you too my heart.

The world broke my neck once
when as a zealous youth
I tried to break new ground
trading vision for wealth.
I drain thinking of you
getting your head round facts
my dear in this slippery place.

My old self has grown old
but I gather my wits
each time to reply to
defiance and hard times.
I am for anything
that can enable you
make a graceful breakthrough
the dark night of your soul
my love now that you bear life.

Let the world not break you
my dear fellow penmen
when you have sown no grain
nor ploughed your own furrow.

Take a look at the course
you have dogged like a dog
these many uphill years
without growth without gain
and change course to conquer.

The world bites everyone.
The low fight with the soil
to keep body and soul
together in the stress
to dominate the ground.
The high dream of long life
lost in the woods of self.
The world cracks everyone
red white black and yellow.

More Sinned Against

More sinned against than sinning
I hold high my smoky head
above the din of black sheep.
Though incensed like a hornet,
though on my knees at my age
like a nameless law-breaker
struggling to mend his image,
I cry daily for the moon
to rise above biased thoughts
but you small fry shadow me.

I will continue to sing
of a world more warm and just
though I have been daubed with lies.
I am too old to cross swords
but my strains can strive with you
till the latrine in your mouth
and the maggots in your heart
stop making my children sick.
My tears can start a fire
that can consume your grandeur
and burn everything you own.

Your fingers are stained with blood
yet you stick your sharp tongue out
at people wrestling with death
under your disastrous rule
in this country so startling
and endowed with rare beauty.
I have come to be your prey

in that I steer clear of crime
and sing against bastard rule.
More sinned against than sinning
I hold high my rock-ribbed head
above the row of blacklegs
eaten up with jealousy.

Supreme Sacrifice

At the crack of another day
cadaverous children roll out
from a cavernous pit their home
to do battle with slender means.
The unchanging sun licks their eyes
as they meander through the land dry
in the clutches of cold hunger.

Their parents met a sticky end
under a flint-hearted ruler.
They made the supreme sacrifice
chained like criminals in dark cells
beyond the view of living souls.
Nobody has knowledge of them,
nobody seems keen to know them
save those who give rulers insomnia,
bards with unwavering consciences.

I wish I could soften your heart
and sow seeds of concern in it.
I wish I could touch your conscience
and stand the shame of our country
in a bowl with holes before you.
I feel the needle of your tongue
and think of the days in time past,
days of yore when our forefathers
stilled and satisfied hungry souls.
We too under a sedulous head
can quieten and settle troubled minds.
I wish you could discard politics

to see the ugly face of deceit.
I wish you could dig into yourself
to take in those who die for country.

Unswerving Friend

Hope my unswerving friend
soothes in the light of dark
as I make my way lone
towards my grey compound
thinking of my country
immersed in alcohol.

I have drawn breath these years,
these many deep dark years
trying to kiss the moon
and usher in new friends.
Not one has come to light
yet I husband my name.

Hope my caring friend sighs
watching the sun go down
daily these many years.
I still see hawks and crows
comb the land for carrion.
I pray my friend should live
to beat on all doorways
and solicit hearts true,
hearts that can shatter stones
and subdue wild horses.
I pray the hearts come out
and set out predisposed
to grow a brand new world
serene sane and stainless,
a world where black and white
red and yellow feel one,

a world where strain and hate
give way to soothing strains.

The Yoke of Love

Swear to me with your hearts
wrapped in green red yellow
that the flames of odium
lit in the minds of louts
will not fan out to you
my singular children
when like water I sink.

Swear to me my sidekicks
gathered in this graveyard
where your grandparents sleep.
Swear to me with your hearts
that peace and harmony
will live and eat with you
to deal with any foe
when I come to nothing
like grass shrunk in the sun.

I could quench any time
though the light in my eyes
seems fully charged with life.
So swear to me my hope
deep in your search for truth
at the height of bad blood.
Swear to me now and here
in this boneyard of shame
that the beam in your eyes
will melt our people's hearts.
Smash the fear in my heart.

With bad blood discarded
and good governance born
after sheathing the sword,
you would develop fast
twining round each other
to become leading light
flooding darkness with light
and setting alight wimps.
The days of long ago
die slowly in my mind
as my eyes grow darkish
under the yoke of love
my love for you my flesh.

Light Your Light

Light your light red giant
in this back-breaking place
where one finds no more space
to stand and stare for long
the tombs of one time friends
or chew over the hereafter
of this once forbearing nation.

Light your refreshing light
midnight sun in my heart
in the dead of the night
that I may see right through
the thick walls of sham smiles
and touch the hearts of the distressed
blunted by corruption and greed.

Shine your light in this place
where we pine, rot and die
with tons and tons of goals
that could change our history.
Grey unrest mushrooms in the land
waiting for young men and maidens
passed over in the written law
to hobble bigots with fetters.

If God should swell my days
and let me sing once more
I will pour out my heart
to oil our way through murk
and eat the fruit of our mettle.

If God should give me new muscles
I will take old men and children
where there is no cry of distress.

Light your light great body
in this place of soiled souls
where ceaselessly we weep
in the back seat of sway.
We are not a conquered people
supplicating to make ends meet.
We are a dignified species
striving for freedom and justice.

Torn By Guilt

While birds frolicked from tree to tree
thanking God for their lives
and dogs and cats fought over milk
their eyes bloodshot like sots,
while deer stalkers staggered back home
without a catch that day,
an orphan walked to the market
not far from the graveyard
and sat down on a whitewashed stone
tired and deep in thought.
Hunger tore his insides apart
looking for new spices
to spice its craze for the wretched.

I saw delinquents in yellow
closing in on the waif
at the going down of the sun.
Tears fell in my frail heart
as rain falls in the wet season
when the juvenile gang
the terror of the neighbourhood
clothed with violence attacked.
They chopped off the orphan's noddle
and threw dust in my eyes.
Where they went to I do not know
but I was torn by guilt
standing there unable to help.

I turned a page in my history
tears dripping in my heart.
I tried closing my eagle eyes
to calm down my conscience
but saw instead thick dark forests.
Fury rose in my veins
and time seemed to be motionless.
I turned another page
the history of my duped people
littered with broken dreams.
I turned and walked away bitter
not because I was lame
but because my history still bleeds.

False Bravado

When in the company of thought
I see the nakedness of my people
at the gates of drunken leaders
I feel like a balloon adrift
alone on a tempest-tossed sea,
not sure of any rescue team.

When in the company of mouths
I hear academics babble
unable to plough deep into
the heart of discrimination,
I feel needles of stinging pain
shoot up from my bitter belly.
To depend on lies and deceit
disfigures the face of the land.

I see a conflagration nigh
and a fire of bitterness
burning in the eyes of the bashed.
The false bravado of some dons
in the name of patriotism
cannot bring light to the plundered.

If we cannot love to survive
except by spilling our own blood
for dwarfs to continue ruling
I call on invisible winds,
Stygian unfathomable winds
to sweep us back to our real roots.
What more can I wish dear kinsmen

worse than what I look forward to?

I wait in the skin of my me
for somebody with no face yet,
someone with penetrating dreams
to tie our hearts in one bundle
and intone songs of belonging,
songs to storm the walls of bondage.

Fall Prostrate Brother

You risk eating your own dung
and drinking your own urine
to stop the sprites of freedom
when they come looking for you.
Better to be stripped of power
to be like a dog with two tails
taking pleasure in protecting
than to be adorned with power
to be thrown out like menstrual cloth
when a new dawn breaks tomorrow.

The end of the road is near.
Travellers would soon have rest
and those turning inside out
the offices where you worked
would coin a song and dance about
the bad governance you watered.
You are at the brink of breakdown.
Better to fall prostrate brother
For the wronged to walk over you
than to pass away like a fly.

To keep baking day and night
the bread of disagreement
to keep your place in the state
is not what will free you man
from the fury of those you milk.
Like every political brute
you lay down your countrymen's lives
for your dish of milk and repute.

I cannot swallow your ideas
to gaze at the blood on your hands.

Dark Moments

We all do have dark moments,
moments when the psyche seems lost
and the interminable light
faint in the eye floats in the air.
The mind disrobed goes underground
treading blindly towards night soil.

I can touch my dark moments
in the day and in the night
no matter how scary they are.
I have grown used to their torture
and their music for those who die
as prisoners from emptiness.

Dark moments are part of life
though they create gaping holes
in the heart of the chopping block.
Dark moments have transformed my mind
into a well-watered garden
where most mediocre intellects
and some intellectuals get lost.
I mark my dark moments in strains
wrapped round the thick necks of despots,
strains dredged from memory and home,
strains that urge syphilitic minds
to kiss the temple of knowledge
and fight to sit on the front seat
in the tantalising state craft
monopolized by ungroomed minds.

Blow Invisible Winds

These many years of my life
spent in the heart of power
have been like a walk through thorns.
I hoped to burst into flower
when I clothed myself some years back
with the flint desire to shine
like a hunter's torch in the night
in a country that drives saints crazy.

I braced myself to endure
briers from the ignorant
as I strove to clean their eyes
with drips from deep in the forest.
The erudite, sharp-beaked like hawks
turn pale, blighted by bitterness
as I struggle to scale the hills
and cross the swift running rivers
in my way to what I was before
my heart was chained to that of deceit.

Blow, blow invisible winds,
blow me and my tender heart
worn out by disappointments.
Blow us into the Sahara
where the sun can alleviate us.
Should we be blown back to our roots
no one will recapture our heart
nor push us around like a robot.
Our dignity dead since waking
will resurrect with projectiles

that will one day discover you
in the bunker of your betrayal.

Lost

My heart is grief-stricken
not because youth is gone
but because the land limps
and we glory in this.

My mind is ill at ease
not because I am ill
but because love is dead
and we are contented.

I feel sharp pain inside
not because joy is gone
but because decay reigns
and we clap like zombies.

My spirit is troubled
and my thoughts flow slowly
not because strength is gone
but because you are lost.

You are lost without God
in a world of bloodshed.
Come before you grow thin
eating what kills the heart.

Come closer to the spring
where I have drunk these years.
Neither cults nor the bait
of deism can shield you.

At this sharp end in life
you must not drop a brick.
The repellent accounts
of your fortunes touch me.

You have been on a drip
since the day you ditched God.
I want to pipe you back
to the Lord of your life.

I feel like Hamlet without the Prince
not because I lack self-confidence
but because square pegs in round holes rule
and we celebrate like eccentrics.

In Yahweh's Hands

Yesterday I was brisk
bubbling with brainless rage
ready like wild fire
to burn every dead leaf.
Swallows and weaver birds
gave me the zeal to fly
but the maker of wings
refused to honour them.
I did not bandy words.

Today I am a snail
harassed by mindless age
set like the hungry grave
to feed on my entrails.
The daystar and the moon
give me the zest to live
but the butcher of life
thinks I am for his pot.
I refuse to concede.

I cannot tolerate lies.
The sky will not fall on me
nor the eye of the full moon
grow dim on my high forehead.
The author of live still lives
though this is a starless night,
a pitch-black and creepy night.
I am sick to death of lies
and will not give in to wiles.

Lifeless leaves turn my stomach
though they sometimes melt my heart
when the wind knocks them around.
I cannot give in to dogs
and no mortal can blow out
the fire in my large eyes.
I am in Yahweh's warm hands
in a place you cannot reach
save you cast aside the world.

A Star Sank Here

Many souls in this sphinxlike land
prefer to quench like a candle
in a gusty and murky night
with no monuments left behind
than retreat within for some time
to think well before giving up.

A rising star sank in this place
caught by the terrors of the night
when he was climbing a palm tree
to gather in its mellow fruit.
A brood of rascals burnt his house
and big shots sripped him of his fields.

I feel shame in my whole body
like a stripped maid before strange eyes.
Day after day on my old bed
I think of this place my heart loves
the place where in my infancy
I was nursed at my mother's breasts.

I will do my best to get up
and worm my way to the runnel
across the earth road to brush up
in good time for the good of poets
my new idiom before I leave
for the place my heart cherishes.

A formidable star sank here
where darkness rules and light sorrows.
I will do my best to stand up
and dart to and fro the pale streets
ready to nurture newcomers
for poetry to live on and on.

When Gone

I want no flowers when gone,
no tears when I cease to be.
Only love strains will thrill me
when fate cuts me to ribbons
and worms warm to welcome me.
Only your love for the Lord
and care for one another
will please me in my new home.
No blossoms when I am gone.

Stubbornly for these many years
I have hung on to the image
my forefathers handed to me
on the eve of independence.
It reveals my natural face
the envy of doctored bodies
and is so grand it dumbfounds you.
Nobody, not even a witch
knows how my heart blocks and unblocks
instantly when the chips are down.
Only my God understands me.

I want no fawning when gone,
no lies when I come to dust.
Only candour will thrill me
when destiny breaks my bones
and the earth becomes my bed.
Only your ties with the Lord
and concern for each other
will thrill me when I am gone.
No eulogies when I leave.

Printed in the United States
By Bookmasters